HOME AUTOMATION SECURITY

TABLE OF CONTENTS

ABBREVIATIONS:

ACs: Air Conditioners

AKC: Authenticated Key exchange protocol with key Confirmation

DH: Diffie-Hellman (DH) key exchange protocol

ECC: Elliptic Curve Cryptography

HTTP: Hyper Text Transport Protocol

IDS: Intrusion Detection System

IFTT: If This Then That

IID: IPv6 interface identifier

IP: Internet Protocol

HD: High Definition

HSM: Hardware Security Modules

IoT: Internet of Things

JTAG: Joint Test Action Group

MFA: Multifactor Authentication

MQTT: Message Queue Telemetry Transport Protocol.

OTP: One-Time Password

OWASP: The Open Web Application Security Project

REST API: Representational State Transfer API

RSA: Rivest, Shamir, Adleman algorithm

SGX: Software Guard Extensions

SH: Smart Home

SHA-256: Secure Hash Algorithm 256

SQLI: Structure Query Language Injection injection attacks

SoC: System on a Chip

TCG: Trusted Computing Group

TEEs: Trusted Execution Environments

TPM: Trusted Platform Modules

TVs: Tele Visions

UID: User Identifier

XSS: Cross Site scripting

YAML: Yet Another Markup Language.

CHAPTER 1. SECURE STORAGE AND WEB INTERFACES IN HOME AUTOMATION

Abstract

According to the latest Internet of Things (IoT), Top-10 vulnerabilities list released by "The Open Web Application Security Project (OWASP)", Insecure Interface is number 3 and Insecure Storage is number 7. This chapter emphasizes the data storage by smart appliances in smart homes. This chapter also discusses the privacy, accessibility, integrity, and other security concerns of both local and cloud data stored in smart home appliances. Based on availability, Secure storage is classified into local storage and cloud storage. Based on nature, secure storage is classified into software-based storage and hardware-based storage. In addition to secure storage, this chapter also describes the web interface of smart home devices. Web interfaces provide a user-friendly way to control and monitor various smart devices through web browsers of computers, laptops, and smartphones. I also highlight the key aspects of web interface such as Data Encryption, Input Validation, Real-Time Control, Responsive Design, Notification and Alerts, Security, User-Friendly Design, and Intuitive Navigation.

Keywords: Secure Storage, Web Interfaces, Home Automation, IoT Security, Hardware Based Storage, Software Based Storage, Local Storage, Cloud Storage, Hybrid Storage

1.1 INTRODUCTION

Smart home (SH) appliances can store data, respond to users' prompts, provide feedback to users, and issue alarms based on the data analytics of stored data [2]. The storage of smart home devices is available in different varieties such as local storage, cloud storage, hardware storage, and software storage. The majority of smart home devices use hybrid storage which is a combination of above mention storage. Security is a primary concern in the storage of data generated in smart home appliances. These data also include sensitive pieces of information like encryption keys, personal information, user credentials, and so on. To ensure secure storage, some developers trust hardware-based storage whereas some trust software-based storage with encryption.

Table 1. Storage Example by Device Types

Smart Home Devices	Storage of Data
Smartphones and Tablets	Android phones usually use Google Drive whereas Apple phones use iCloud to sync/ backup local data stored in internal flash memory.
Smart Home Devices:	Google's Nest, Amazon's Ring, and Samsung's SmartThings
Wearables:	Fitness trackers and smartwatches store activity data locally and upload it to cloud services (e.g., Fitbit, Apple Health).
Smart Appliances:	Smart ACs, smart refrigerators, or Smart washing machines store usage data locally and also sync with the manufacturer's cloud service for remote technical support.

Android smartphones use Google Drive [3]. Apple smartphones use iCloud. Most Smart home devices use either Amazon Ring or Google Nest to sync data on the Cloud [4]. According to OWASP Mobile Top 10 [5], insecure data storage is one of the leading top 10 security issues in smartphones in 2016 and 2024 as shown in Table. 2. It means that sensitive information can be revealed if not protected carefully.

Table 2. Comparison of OWASP Mobile Top 10 in 2016 and 2024

OWASP Mobile Top 10		
2016	2024	Comparison
M1: Improper Platform Usage	M1: Improper Credential Usage	New
M2: Insecure Data Storage	M2: Inadequate Supply Chain Security	New
M3: Insecure Communication	M3: Insecure Authentication/Authorization	Merged M4&M6 to M3
M4: Insecure Authentication	M4: Insufficient Input/Output Validation	New
M5: Insufficient Cryptography	M5: Insecure Communication	Moved from M3 to M5
M6: Insecure Authorization	M6: Inadequate Privacy Controls	New
M7: Client Code Quality	M7: Insufficient Binary Protection	Merged M8&M9 to M7
M8: Code Tampering	M8: Security Misconfiguration	Rewording M10
M9: Reverse Engineering	M9: Insecure Data Storage	Moved from M2 to M9
M10: Extraneous Functionality	M10: Insufficient Cryptography	Moved from M5 5o M10

Google's Nest, Amazon's Ring, and Samsung's SmartThings are three major brands in the smart home industry, each offering a range of products designed to enhance home automation, security, and convenience as shown in Table 3.

Table 3. Comparison of Product Line up of 3 Players in the Smart Home Industry

Nest	Ring	SmartThings
Nest Thermostat	Ring Doorbells	SmartThings Hub
Nest Cameras	Ring Cameras	SmartThings Sensors
Nest Hello Doorbell	Ring Alarm System	SmartThings Outlets
Nest Protect	Ring Smart Lighting	SmartThings Cameras
Nest Hub		

SmartThings Sensors are a set of Motion sensors, multipurpose sensors, and water leak sensors that trigger automation and alerts. Either SmartThings hub or Net Hub connects and controls a wide range of smart devices, including lights, locks, sensors, and cameras as shown in Table 2. Similarly, either SmartThings outlets or Ring smart lighting are smart plugs that control lights and appliances remotely. The cameras provided by Nest, Ring, and SmartThings are security cameras monitoring and recording activities in and around the home. The Doorbell offered by Nest and Ring provides high-definition (HD) Videos of the visitor on the main gate.

1.2 SECURE STORAGE

To achieve the goal of secure storage, smart devices either use hardware-based secure storage if the budget is not a primary concern and security is of paramount importance otherwise software-based secure storage is more economical in comparison to hardware-based secure storage. In addition to hardware and software-based storage, storage is also classified into local and cloud-based storage solutions. Smart devices store data using a combination of local and cloud-based storage solutions. The specifics depend on the device type, its intended use, and the manufacturer's design.

A. Hardware-Based Secure Storage

Hardware-based secure storage is possible with the usage of any of two hardware devices namely Trusted Platform Modules (TPM) and Hardware Security Modules (HSM). There are a few more hardware solutions like a trusted execution environment inside the processor to achieve the goal of hardware-based secure storage. The Trusted Platform Module (TPM) is a microchip (miniature System on a Chip (SoC)) developed by the Trusted Computing Group (TCG) that enhances the integrity of computing platforms. Additionally, it offers secure storage for small amounts of sensitive data, such as cryptographic keys. TPMs also perform Cryptographic operations such as Asymmetric key generation, data encryption, digital signing, Key migration between TPMs, random number generation, and hashing as shown in Fig. 1.1. The primary goal of the TPM is to establish a hardware-based root of trust for computing platforms, providing a higher level of tamper resistance compared to software-based trusted computing bases [6]. The TPM is used in smart home devices to protect encryption keys, financial information, and credentials for authentication.

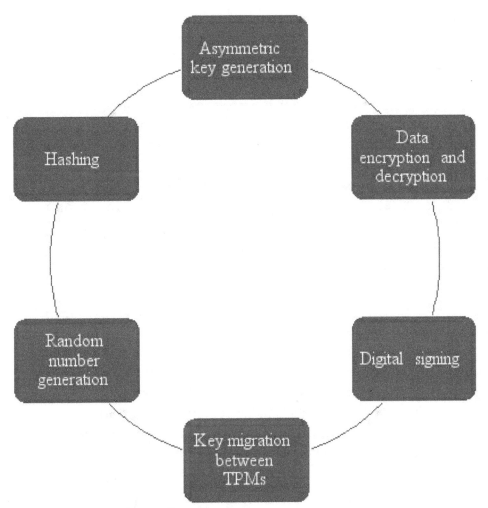

Fig. 1.1. Cryptographic Operations of TPM

Once keys are generated, they must be stored securely. Hardware security modules (HSM) are commonly used to protect the confidentiality of keys [7]. The primary usage of HSM is for centralized security management in IoT gateways and hubs. Trusted Execution Environments (TEEs) are secure areas of central processors or devices that execute code with higher security than the rest of the device. They provide confidentiality and integrity for sensitive data in all its states. TEEs are similar to hardware security modules but are a component of the typical chipset rather than a separate dedicated device [7]. Full Disk encryption is also a hardware-based security scheme [7]. Hardware Security Modules (HSM) is a dedicated hardware device that offers physical protection by integrating a new security layer into the system architecture. When HSM is integrated with decentralized access technologies such as Blockchain, HSM offers robustness and secure end-to-end mechanisms for authenticity, authorization, and integrity [8].

B. Software-Based Secure Storage

Encrypted storage and Secure enclaves are the two most common ways of software-based secure storage. Encryption of Full Disk or Encrypted Storage is a way of software-based secure storage where we encrypt all data before being stored in memory or on disk. In this scenario, data is unreadable without the decryption key. This is a very promising way to protect data stored on smart home appliances even if the device is compromised then also data is secured. Researchers in [9], proposed an encrypted storage model based on the MedGreen communication authentication scheme and MedSecrecy algorithm. Secure Enclaves are isolated execution environments within the main processor to ensure data and code are protected from unauthorized access. Secure enclaves such as Intel Software Guard Extensions (SGX) an isolated execution environments that provide a guarantee of the privacy of the data/code deployed inside it [10]. Just like SGX in Intel, ARM Trust Zone is also a Secure Enclave in ARM processors.

C. Local Storage:

Internal memory, external memory, and cache memory are the local storage used by smart devices in smart homes. Many smart home devices (like TVs, cameras, doorbells, sensors, thermostats, and so on), have built-in flash memory or hard drives to store data. This includes operating system files, firmware, middleware, application data, user preferences, and locally generated data (e.g., photos, videos, logs, or any multimedia types). Some smart home devices support external storage options, such as SD cards or USB drives, to expand storage capacity. This is common in devices like smart cameras, smartphones, smart TVs, and other smart appliances. Devices like smart assistants (e.g., Amazon Echo, Google Home) use cache memory to temporarily store data for quick access, improving performance and responsiveness.

D. Cloud Storage:

Cloud Services like Google Drive, iCloud, Nest, Ring, SmartThings, etc. are used by various smart devices for both data storage and sync data to ensure availability across multiple devices and remote access. Smart security cameras store video footage in the cloud and smart assistants store voice recordings and user interactions in cloud databases are examples of data storage in the cloud. Smartphones sync photos, contacts, and application data with cloud services like Google Drive, iCloud, or OneDrive are an example of sync data with cloud. In addition to storage, and syncing, cloud-based storage is also used by smart home appliances for the backup of data to prevent data loss in case the device is damaged or lost. As data stored on the cloud is easy to modify and delete, the data owner faces many security issues like unauthorized access, tampering with data, and losing control of their data [11].

E. Hybrid Storage:

Smart devices have to store some data locally for fast access and to preserve privacy and some data on the cloud due to the limitation of local memory in smart devices. Therefore, I observed that the majority of smart home appliances use hybrid storage. Some smart devices use edge computing, where data processing and storage occur close to the data source (the "edge" of the network). Edge computing reduces latency and saves bandwidth as data is locally processed and only sends essential information to the cloud. Researchers in [12] proposed a cost-effective integrated system for smart homes based on IoT and Edge Computing. Their proposed system provides security, safety, and remote control. Their proposed system also stores sensitive data in a local cloud to preserve privacy. Data are processed on edge to reduce bandwidth. Many smart home devices use a combination of local and cloud storage to optimize performance and reliability. For instance, a smart thermostat might store recent temperature data locally for quick access and periodically sync with the cloud for long-term storage and analysis.

1.3 WEB INTERFACES IN HOME AUTOMATION

Web interfaces play a pivotal role in smart home, providing a user-friendly way to control and monitor various smart home appliances with web browsers on various computers, laptops, and smartphones. Data Encryption, Input Validation, Intuitive Navigation, Real-Time Control, Responsive Design, Notification and Alerts, Security, User-Friendly Design, and Visual feedback are the main key aspects of Web Interfaces are shown in Fig. 11.2.

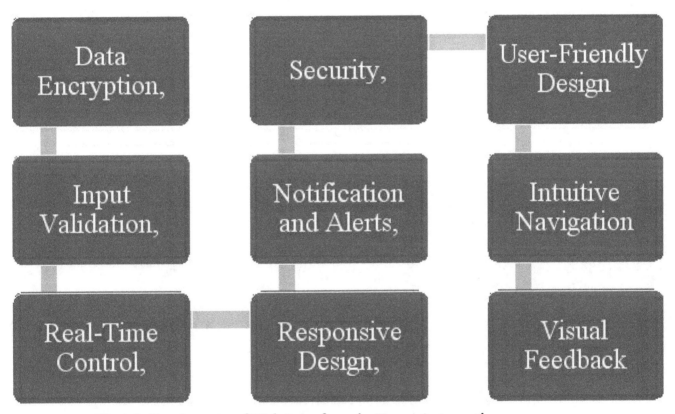

Fig 1.2. Key Aspects of Web Interfaces in Home Automation

The web interface of smart home devices must have security features like input validation so there will be no possibility to perform Structure Query Language Injection (SQLI) injection attacks and cross-site scripting (XSS). Other security features of the web interface must be session management, data encryption, authentication, and authorization. Attacks via the web interface. The user interface and User Experience of the Web Interface should feel good and user-friendly. The web interface should work seamlessly across different screen sizes and different browsers. There should be visual feedback in the web interface in the form of visual indicators and real-time updates. There are many more optional features in the web interface such as real-time control of view and monitoring dashboard, notifications and alerts, customization and routine setup, integration with other services like Alexa and Google Assistant, and device management. The web interface will be rated better if it has a Centralized dashboard displaying the status and control options for multiple devices. Real-time alerts for important events like security breaches or device malfunctions must integrated into the web interface. In an ideal web interface, Users can create custom scenes and routines to automate their smart home. The web interface should be able to integrate with third-party services like IFTTT or voice assistants like Alexa and Google Assistant. Easy addition or deletion of devices within the home automation system should be available in the web interface. Last but not least, there should be an interface for updating device firmware to ensure security and functionality.

1.4 EXAMPLES OF WEB INTERFACES:

In [13], the researcher illustrated the User Interface of TP-Link Devices in OpenHAB and the User Interface of LG LK54 Smart TV in OpenHAB. In [14], the researcher illustrated the Web Interface of Adding a Network Camera in the Home Assistant. Here, I have taken the example of a user interface of Panasonic AC using MirAIe as shown in Fig. 3. The MirAIe app shows the room temperature of the living room as 25 degrees Celsius. There is also a user interface for universal projector remote control apps as shown in Fig. 4. This App shows the projector model and saved remote. In addition to OpenHAB and Home Assistant, there are many other open-source home automation platforms with functional web interfaces such as Domoticz, Calaos, Jeedom, Fhem, and toggle. However, Open HAB is developed in Java and Home Assistant is developed in Python [15]. Whereas both OpenHAB and Home Assistant use the same API called Representational state transfer (REST).

Fig. 1. 3 User Interface of Panasonic AC in MirAIe

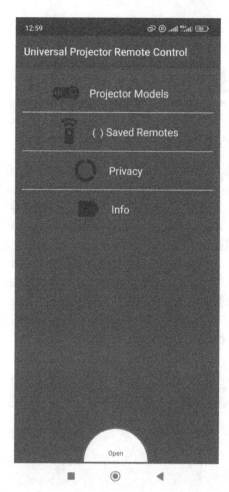

Fig. 1. 4 User Interface of Universal Projector Remote Control

1.5 CONCLUSION

Web interfaces in home automation IoT systems are essential for providing users with an accessible, secure, and efficient way to manage their smart homes. They enable real-time control and monitoring, customization of automation, and seamless integration with other services, ensuring a user-friendly and powerful smart home experience. Storage is managed by appliances in smart homes both locally and syncing with the cloud. Google Drive and iCloud are the most popular ones. Whereas, each manufacturer has its own cloud services like Nest of Google, Ring of Amazon, SmartThings of Samsung, and so on. Data stored locally or transmitted to the cloud is encrypted to prevent unauthorized access. Only users with passwords, biometrics, or two-factor authentication have access to data storage. To hide the identity of the user, data is anonymized to ensure privacy.

REFERENCES

[1] OWASP IoT 10 2018, Last Accessed on 23 June 2024 https://wiki.owasp.org/index.php/OWASP_Internet_of_Things_Project

[2] Caldera, M., Hussain, A., Romano, S., & Re, V. (2023). Energy-consumption pattern-detecting technique for household appliances for smart home platform. *Energies*, *16*(2), 824.

[3] Haya Altuwaijri, Sanaa Ghouzali, (2020). Android data storage security: A review, Journal of King Saud University - Computer and Information Sciences, 32(5), 543-552, https://doi.org/10.1016/j.jksuci.2018.07.004.

[4] Wilkinson, J. S. (2020). The Internet of Things. In Communication Technology Update and Fundamentals (pp. 277-289). Routledge.

[5] OWASP Mobile Top 10 2024, Last Accessed on 23 June 2024   https://owasp.org/www-project-mobile-top-10/

[6] Lu, D., Han, R., Shen, Y., Dong, X., Ma, J., Du, X., & Guizani, M. (2020). xTSeH: A trusted platform module sharing scheme towards smart IoT-eHealth devices. *IEEE Journal on Selected Areas in Communications*, *39*(2), 370-383.

[7] Sommerhalder, M. (2023). Hardware Security Module. *Trends in Data Protection and Encryption Technologies*, 83-87.

[8] Cabrera-Gutiérrez, A. J., Castillo, E., Escobar-Molero, A., Álvarez-Bermejo, J. A., Morales, D. P., & Parrilla, L. (2022). Integration of hardware security modules and permissioned blockchain in industrial iot networks. *IEEE Access*, *10*, 114331-114345.

[9] Zhang, J., Liu, H., & Ni, L. (2020). A secure energy-saving communication and encrypted storage model based on RC4 for EHR. *Ieee Access*, *8*, 38995-39012.

[10] Elgamal, T., & Nahrstedt, K. (2020, May). Serdab: An IoT framework for partitioning neural networks computation across multiple enclaves. In *2020 20th IEEE/ACM International Symposium on Cluster, Cloud and Internet Computing (CCGRID)* (pp. 519-528). IEEE.

[11] Ren, Y., Leng, Y., Qi, J., Sharma, P. K., Wang, J., Almakhadmeh, Z., & Tolba, A. (2021). Multiple cloud storage mechanism based on blockchain in smart homes. *Future Generation Computer Systems*, *115*, 304-313.

[12] Yar, H., Imran, A. S., Khan, Z. A., Sajjad, M., & Kastrati, Z. (2021). Towards smart home automation using IoT-enabled edge-computing paradigm. *Sensors*, *21*(14), 4932.

[13] Parocha, R. C., & Macabebe, E. Q. B. (2019, November). Implementation of home automation system using OpenHAB framework for heterogeneous IoT devices. In *2019 IEEE International Conference on Internet of Things and Intelligence System (IoTaIS)* (pp. 67-73). IEEE.

[14] Akhmetzhanov, B. K., Gazizuly, O. A., Nurlan, Z., & Zhakiyev, N. (2022, April). Integration of a video surveillance system into a smart home using the home assistant platform. In *2022 International Conference on Smart Information Systems and Technologies (SIST)* (pp. 1-5). IEEE.

[15] Stolojescu-Crisan, C., Crisan, C., & Butunoi, B. P. (2021). An IoT-based smart home automation system. Sensors, 21(11), 3784.

CHAPTER 2: SECURE SOFTWARE AND FIRMWARE IN HOME AUTOMATION: INSECURE FIRMWARE IS AN EVIL MAID

Abstract

The smart home provides homeowners with unmatched and unique comfort and control. Smart switches, smart lights, smart TVs (televisions), smart ACs (Air Conditioners), Smart music players, smart gas and water sensors, switching off the power, and water geysers make the smart home a more power-optimized home. All smart appliances need software and firmware to regulate them and get the highest performance from the hardware. This chapter surveyed the most popular 12 firmware and 4 software used in home automation. During our literature survey, I also observed that common people are interested in buying smart appliances but do not know how to update firmware and software. Failing to update software and firmware is one of the most common vulnerabilities in smart home security. Even if firmware is updated on time, the lack of a secure update mechanism is another common vulnerability where hackers may modify or upload malicious firmware. In the end, I have done three case studies of uses of the smart kettle in My Kitchen in Astana Kazakhstan, the smart AC in My Living room in Greater Noida India, and the smart Projection in the classroom of Astana IT University, Kazakhstan.

Keywords: Secure Software, Secure Firmware, Firmware Vulnerability, Home Automation, IoT Security

2.1 INTRODUCTION

Domestic home appliances such as Smart TVs, Smart Refrigerators, Smart ACs, Smart Water Heaters, and Smart Plugs are the most common appliances in Smart Homes. Some sensors for monitoring humidity, environmental temperature, movement, and gases are examples of IoT sensors in smart homes [1]. Common people are interested in buying smart devices but they are not committing their time to updating firmware and software. The non-regular update of software and firmware is one of the most common vulnerabilities in the security of home automation [2]. To solve this common problem, researchers developed qToggle to facilitate the updating of device firmware of different types and models [3]. The smart home appliances consist of sensors and software/firmware so they automatically communicate with other appliances or controllers. However, the sellers of smart home appliances do not disclose information about firmware specifications. This makes common buyers suffer from poor purchases. In [4], the researcher proposed the idea of a firmware label and expects this label will be shown on the packaging of appliances to inform customers about firmware. In [5], researchers proposed a model called UP-Home that continuously monitors the smart home devices' software stack (e.g., applications, middleware, operating system, firmware) and updates this stack so that smart home devices will not be hacked with known vulnerabilities and exploits. In Fig. 1, there are many security issues with firmware, like Uploading malicious firmware, not updating firmware, lack of secure update mechanism, and inability to stop modifying a device's firmware. Above all, the lack of physical reinforcement that cannot be added with a software update is also a major concern in firmware security. In [6], researchers recognize firmware analysis as the most important part of smart home security assessments. They identify security concerns other than the timely update of firmware as shown in Fig. 2.1. Also, they enlist the three ways of extracting firmware such as bus sniffing, firmware dumping, and reverse engineering. Embedded system vendors do not publish their firmware to safeguard their own Internet Protocol (IP) or limit access to it. That's why, we have to use debug ports (e.g., Joint Test Action Group (JTAG)), and Universal Serial Bus (USB) ports manually to extract or dump firmware from smart home appliances [7].

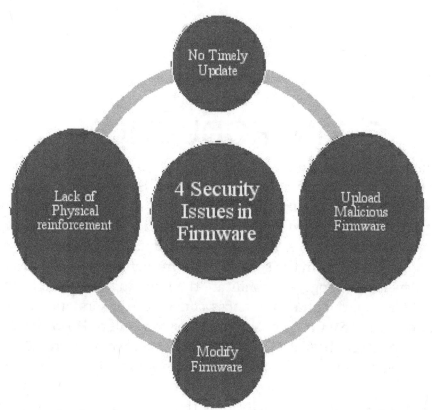

Fig. 2.1. Security Issues in Firmware

Emulation is a cost-effective way as there is no need for the development of hardware. Emulation of smart home appliances will accelerate the discovery and mitigation of vulnerabilities in smart home appliance firmware and therefore become an emerging research area in vulnerability research and analysis of firmware [8]. Tasmota, ESPHome, OpenWrt, Homebridge, Tizen, Hubitat, SmartThings, Zigbee2MQTT, Z-Wave, Deconz, Sonoff, and MySensors are the most popular firmware used in home automation as shown in Fig. 2. 2.

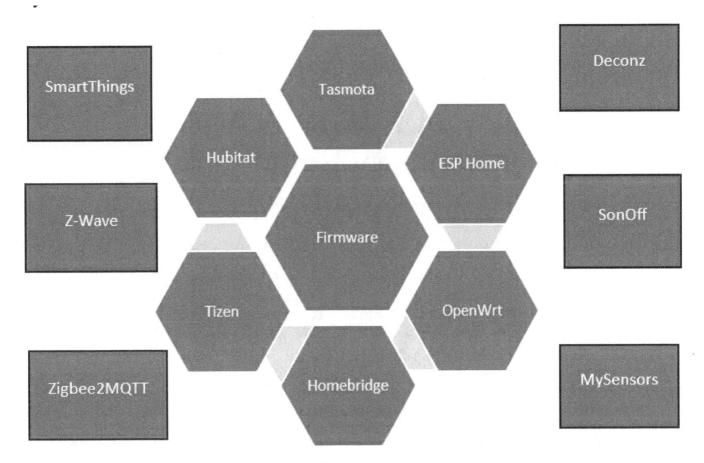

Fig. 2.2. Various Firmware in Home Automation

2.2 CODE AUDITS AND VULNERABILITY ASSESSMENTS ON FIRMWARE

Code audits are not a testing of code functionality but a search of vulnerabilities. There is a vulnerability-oriented fuzzing tool named FIRMCORN. The FIRMCORN tool is using a vulnerable-code search algorithm to find vulnerabilities in IoT firmware [9]. In [10], researchers provide a solution for various stakeholders in the smart home to test the compliance of their devices and audit various firmware components. In their research, they integrate both static vulnerability assessment and dynamic vulnerability assessment. Static analysis audited hard-coded passwords, memory protection bugs, obsolete modules, and so on. Dynamic vulnerability assessment evaluated open ports, unstable networks, and insecure firmware update processes. To pass Code Audits for firmware, the firmware developer must follow secure coding practices and frameworks (e.g., OWASP (OWASP: The Open Web Application Security Project) Secure Coding Practices [11]) as shown in Following Table 1.

Table 1: OWASP Internet of Things (IoT) Top 10 2014

I1 Insecure Web Interface
I2 Insufficient Authentication/Authorization
I3 Insecure Network Services
I4 Lack of Transport Encryption
I5 Privacy Concerns
I6 Insecure Cloud Interface
I7 Insecure Mobile Interface
I8 Insufficient Security Configurability
I9 Insecure Software/Firmware
I10 Poor Physical Security

An insecure Web Interface is the top vulnerability. Insufficient Authentication/Authorization is the second in the Top 10 list of IoT vulnerabilities. Poor physical security is number 10 in the list of top 10 IoT Vulnerabilities ranking released by the Open Web Application Security Project (OWASP).

2.3 HOME AUTOMATION SOFTWARE

Many Androids and iOS applications are used by common people to regulate devices in smart homes. I am adding only two devices: a water heater from the kitchen from Dr Bishwajeet Pandey and a Panasonic AC from the living room of Dr Bishwajeet Pandey.

A. Mi Smart Home APP and Hacking Firmware of Mi Smart Kettle

Mi Smart Kettle has two buttons: Boil and Keep Warm as shown in Fig. 2.3. The Mi Smart Kettle is connected by Bluetooth. To connect with the App, the Keep Warm button should be held down for more than three seconds. After connecting the Mi Home App [12], the real temperature of the water in the kettle will be displayed in the App. The thermal insulation temperature will also be displayed in the app, which I can customize using the App.

Fig. 2.3. Mi Smart Kettle with Wireless Connection Bluetooth 4.0 BLE in the Kitchen of Astana, Kazakhstan

CASE STUDY:

Aleksah in [19] acquired a Mi Smart Kettle Pro. This smart kettle is a Bluetooth-enabled kettle with a companion smartphone app. Despite its advanced features, the kettle couldn't be switched on or off remotely. He believed in his smart home, he should be able to start the kettle right as he woke up, and he decided to solve this problem. Initially, he disassembled the kettle intending to dump the firmware, modify it, and restore it. This seemed straightforward, but there was a complication. The kettle uses a QN9022 controller from the QN902X family of chips as shown in Fig. 5. The QN9020 and QN9021 controllers of the same microcontroller family consist of an internal flash memory similar to the ESP8285. The QN9022 is made of an external SPI flash memory. Generally, dumping the firmware is as simple as reading the flash chip. But, dumping the firmware becomes more complex when the firmware is encrypted with a unique key stored internally in the MCU. As the microcontroller reads the flash chip's contents, they are decrypted transparently before execution. Here, the MCU is accessing the decryption key. He is using the SWD interface. The SWD interface is a powerful and commonly used debug interface for accessing internal data on many MCUs. Unfortunately, this microcontroller has blocked SWD access at the time of manufacturing. Although not every manufacturer sets these bits, he checked the SWD interface just in case, but it was unresponsive. Thus, he took a different approach. He searched and got the MCU's internal bootloader and planned to load his code into RAM to dump the flash contents from within. The read command inside the bootloader either scrambles or erases the flash, resulting in a dead unit. He tries to dump the bootloader code with other RAM stuff. He discovered a few undocumented but unimportant commands during the decompiling of the bootloader. Crucially, he learned that loading any program causes the bootloader to send a command to the flash chip to perform an erase. At this point, he considered using a tweezer hack to write-protect the flash by short-circuiting its data pins. However, he decided to seek a proper dumping method that would also work for chips with built-in flash, should one of those come across his desk in the future. His key discovery came soon afterward. The bootloader detects a vulnerable structure that allows modification of these commands to match the specific flash chip connected. By replacing the flash erase command in that vulnerable structure with a harmless one, he was able to keep the flash contents intact, even after loading new code externally into RAM [19]. As a result, Aleksah developed a methodology for dumping encrypted firmware from any QN902X series MCU using USB-UART, chip bootloader, and a dumping tool (available on GitHub: https://github.com/a-sakharov/qn902x-dump)

B. MIRAIe Secure IoT Home Automation Software and Updating AC Firmware

I have a Panasonic AC installed in Greater Noida, India. Using MiRAIe, AC can be ON or OFF not only from anywhere in India but also from my office in Astana, Kazakhstan as shown in Fig. 2.4. I can go to settings and update firmware as shown in Fig. 2.5.

11:26 M …

Good Morning
32.4°C Rain

You can create the AC sleep profile using an
interactive graphical view from the AC details
page

A-107

My Living Room
1 Device

PANASONIC AC

25°C

❄
Cool

Fig. 2.4. On/OFF AC in India from Any Corner of Earth

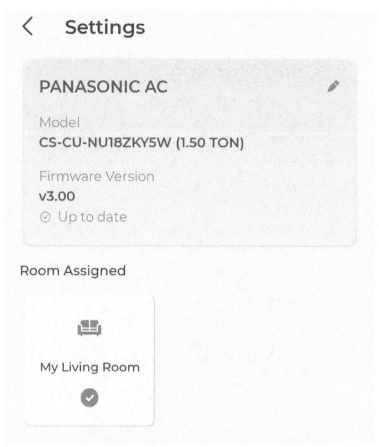

Fig. 2.5. Updating Firmware in Smart Mi Kettle

C. Universal Projector Remote Control and Updating Firmware of EPSON Projector

The application Universal Projector Remote Control is used to open any Projector in our classroom. Here, I ON the projector of Epson as shown in Fig. 2.6a, 2.6b, and 2.6c.

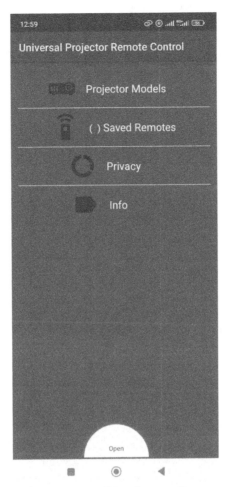

Fig.2. 6a Main Screen of Projector Remote Control

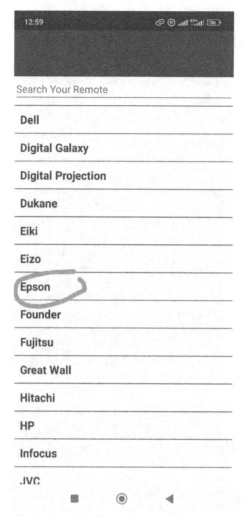

Fig. 2.6b Select Projector Model (Here Epson)

We can update the projector's firmware using a USB storage device or a computer and a USB cable. If a firmware update is available for our projector model, we can select the Firmware Update option in the projector's Initial/All Settings menu. The projector will enter firmware update mode and be ready to perform a firmware update. If a firmware update file is not found, the projector will enter standby mode. We can download the firmware update file from our product's support page [20].

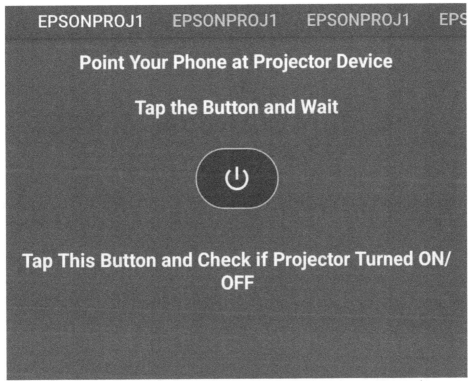

EPSONPROJ1   EPSONPROJ1   EPSONPROJ1   EPS

Point Your Phone at Projector Device

Tap the Button and Wait

Tap This Button and Check if Projector Turned ON/ OFF

Fig.2.6c Turned ON Projector Model (Here EpsonPROJ1)

2.4 FIRMWARE IN HOME AUTOMATION

The primary purpose of home automation is to increase convenience. The secondary purpose of home automation is both security and energy efficiency. Firmware is a low-level software that controls the hardware of a smart home. Therefore, I conclude that Firmware is an enabler to achieve both the primary and secondary purpose of home automation. Table 2 is a list of some popular firmware such as ESPHome, Homebridge, HUbitat, OpenWrt, Smart Things, Tasmota, Tizen, Z-Wave, and Zigbee2MQTT used in home automation with the elaboration of Purpose, Features and Use Cases. YAML is Yet Another Markup Language. MQTT is an acronym for Message Queue Telemetry Transport Protocol.

Table 2: Comparative Studies of Popular Firmware in Home Automation

	Purpose	Features	Use Cases
ESPHome [13]	Usable with ESP8266 and ESP32 devices Integrable with Home Assistant	• YAML-based configuration, • Extensive device support, • OTA updates, • Smart integration with Home Assistant.	Lights, sensors, switches, climate control
Homebridge [14]	Acts as a bridge between Homekit and numerous non-Homekit smart home devices.	• Extensible through community plugins • Wide Range of Plugin, • Written in Node.js	Integrating non-HomeKit devices with Apple HomeKit ecosystem.
Hubitat Elevation [15]	Used with Hubitat home automation platform	• Local processing, • Wide device support • Advanced automation rules.	The central hub for managing various smart devices, and automation controllers.
OpenWrt [16]	Mainly used for	• Highly	Gateways,

	routers	• Customizable Robust Network and Security Features	IoT Hubs, and Routers
SmartThings [17]	Samsung's proprietary firmware for its SmartThings hub and devices. Features	• Cloud and local processing, • Extensive device ecosystem, • Automation and scene control	Smart home hubs, lights, sensors, cameras.
Tasmota	Used with ESP8266 and ESP8285 compatible devices.	• Customizable • Support A Wide range of sensors • MQTT Protocols for Communications • OTA Updates	Smart plugs, lights, sensors, and switches.
Tizen	Samsung smart home appliances	• Extensive API for Appliances control • Lightweight • Support Web Applications	Smart Refrigerators Smart TVs Smart Watches
Zigbee2MQTT [18]	Allows Zigbee devices to communicate with MQTT servers	• Zigbee devices, • Integrate with home automation platforms like Home Assistant	Zigbee smart bulbs, sensors, switches.
Z-Wave Firmware	Used with Z-Wave devices and controllers	• Secure communication, • Mesh network, • Extensive device support	Smart locks, lights, thermostats, sensors.

In addition to the 9 Firmware discussed in Table 2, there are many other firmware like Deconz, Sonoff, MySensors, and so forth.

2.5 CONCLUSION

These firmware in smart home appliances are similar to the backbone of the human body. This firmware helps smart home devices to perform and integrate seamlessly into smart homes. If we update firmware regularly and can check malicious firmware then secure smart home is not a distant reality. Each firmware has its unique pros and cons and is suitable for various types of smart home devices and use cases.

REFERENCES

[1] Bhardwaj, A., Kaushik, K., Alshehri, M., Mohamed, A. A. B., & Keshta, I. (2023). ISF: Security analysis and assessment of smart home IoT-based firmware. *ACM Transactions on Sensor Networks*.

[2] Khalid, A., Rahman, N. A. A., & Shajaratuddur, K. (2024). Secure IoT based Home Automation by Identifying Vulnerabilities and Threats. *Digital Innovation Adoption: Architectural Recommendations and Security Solutions*, 40.

[3] Stolojescu-Crisan, C., Crisan, C., & Butunoi, B. P. (2021). An IoT-based smart home automation system. *Sensors*, *21*(11), 3784.

[4] Rajkhan, N. W., & Song, J. (2021, December). IoT Smart Home Devices' Security, Privacy, and Firmware Labeling System. In *2021 International Conference on Computational Science and Computational Intelligence (CSCI)* (pp. 1874-1880). IEEE.

[5] Silva, J., Rosa, N., & Aires, F. (2024). UP-Home: A Self-Adaptive Solution for Smart Home Security. *Journal of Universal Computer Science (JUCS)*, *30*(4).

[6] Murat, K., Topyła, D., Zdulski, K., Marzęcki, M., Bieniasz, J., Paczesny, D., & Szczypiorski, K. (2024). Security Analysis of Low-Budget IoT Smart Home Appliances Embedded Software and Connectivity. *Electronics*, *13*(12), 2371.

[7] Qasem, A., Shirani, P., Debbabi, M., Wang, L., Lebel, B., & Agba, B. L. (2021). Automatic vulnerability detection in embedded devices and firmware: Survey and layered taxonomies. *ACM Computing Surveys (CSUR)*, *54*(2), 1-42.

[8] Wright, C., Moeglein, W. A., Bagchi, S., Kulkarni, M., & Clements, A. A. (2021). Challenges in firmware re-hosting, emulation, and analysis. *ACM Computing Surveys (CSUR)*, *54*(1), 1-36.

[9] Bakhshi, T., Ghita, B., & Kuzminykh, I. (2024). A Review of IoT Firmware Vulnerabilities and Auditing Techniques. *Sensors*, *24*(2), 708.

[10] Kagita, M. K., Bojja, G. R., & Kaosar, M. (2021). A framework for intelligent IoT firmware compliance testing. *Internet of Things and Cyber-Physical Systems*, *1*, 1-7.

[11] OWASP Internet of Things Project, Last Accessed on 23 June 2024 https://wiki.owasp.org/index.php/OWASP_Internet_of_Things_Project#tab=IoT_Top_10

[12] Mi Smart Kettle, https://www.lazada.com.ph/products/xiaomi-mi-smart-electric-kettle-pro-1800w-fast-boiling-15l-stainless-steel-with-led-digital-screen-and-app-control-via-bluetooth-modelmjhwsh02ym-white-i2380775765.html

[13] Gozuoglu, A., Ozgonenel, O., & Gezegin, C. (2024). Design and Implementation of Controller Boards to Monitor and Control Home Appliances for Future Smart Homes. IEEE Transactions on Industrial Informatics.

[14] Ma, X., Zeng, Q., Chi, H., & Luo, L. (2023, June). No More Companion Apps Hacking but One Dongle: Hub-Based Blackbox Fuzzing of IoT Firmware. In Proceedings of the 21st Annual International Conference on Mobile Systems, Applications and Services (pp. 205-218).

[15] Device Firmware Updater, https://docs2.hubitat.com/en/apps/device-firmware-updater

[16] Zhao, B., Ji, S., Xu, J., Tian, Y., Wei, Q., Wang, Q., ... & Beyah, R. (2022, July). A large-scale empirical analysis of the vulnerabilities introduced by third-party components in IoT firmware.

In Proceedings of the 31st ACM SIGSOFT International Symposium on Software Testing and Analysis (pp. 442-454).

[17] Knapp, A., Wamuo, E., Rahat, M. A., Torres-Arias, S., Bloom, G., & Zhuang, Y. (2024, January). Should Smart Homes Be Afraid of Evil Maids?: Identifying Vulnerabilities in IoT Device Firmware. In 2024 IEEE 14th Annual Computing and Communication Workshop and Conference (CCWC) (pp. 0467-0473). IEEE.

[18] Hussein, N., & Nhlabatsi, A. (2022). Living in the dark: Mqtt-based exploitation of iot security vulnerabilities in zigbee networks for smart lighting control. IoT, 3(4), 450-472.

[19] Hacking Mi Smart Kettle Firmware, Last Accessed on 25 June 2024 https://hackaday.com/2022/05/04/dumping-encrypted-at-rest-firmware-of-xiaomi-smart-kettle/

[20] Epson Projector Firmware, Last Accessed on 25 June 2024 https://files.support.epson.com/docid/cpd6/cpd61218/source/maintenance/concepts/projector_firmware_update_download.html

CHAPTER 3: IDENTITY-BASED AUTHENTICATION, ENCRYPTION, AND DIGITAL SIGNATURES

Abstract

The smart home is the latest technology in the field of ubiquitous computing to manage devices at smart homes using the internet or bluetooth. To confirm that Real users are accessing data, the smart home system will authenticate users using passwords, cookies, session ID key exchange authentication, multifactor authentication, and so on. Encryption, self-sign certificates, certificates signed by certification authorities, and Digital signatures also play a major role in creating a secure home.

Keywords: Identity, Authentication, Encryption, Digital Signatures, Web Security, IoT Security

3.1 INTRODUCTION

The smart home without an authentication mechanism will face multiple security issues. When we go with the traditional approach of authentication it will not deliver the required security and performance. Traditionally, there are Hyper Text Transport Protocol (HTTP) Basic Authentication, and HTTP Digest Authentication available with a conventional login form. Basic Authentication is insecure when transmitted over unencrypted channels, while Digest Authentication is unnecessarily complicated and requires exchanging multiple messages. That's why in this chapter, we are exploring other possible ways of authentication in addition to these two traditional ways of authentication. Of late, multiple authentication protocols have been developed to verify the user's identity and ensure that the data or device is accessed with authorization in the smart home. Whenever we download software to control and monitor smart devices in smart homes, users must give their consent before using the application. Usually, applications want to get consent to collect personal information, like giving access to contacts, calls, cameras, locations, and so on. If the user does not give consent then the application will not operate. Users are forced to give consent to the collection of personal information, which means that personal privacy may be exposed at any time [1]. When common people buy smart home appliances they should change the default password without delay. There is an urgent need to change the default passwords of smart home appliances as there are many default password databases. Otherwise, hackers may get the default password from the database and compromise smart home appliances. Whenever we are changing the default password, we have to also ensure that we are using a strong password. Otherwise, the weak password will easily be cracked by any brute-force attack with the help of a word list of common passwords. In place of centralized password verification, smart home devices are also using key exchange-based authentication where several sensors and devices in smart homes together verify the correctness of the user password. There are many internet services like IFTT (If This Then That) that integrate heterogeneous Smart Home devices and allow the user to customize smart home configuration via IFTTT recipes. Sensor-based IoT devices such as smart ACs, bulbs, doorbells, plugs, switches, speakers, and smart TVs allow users to control everything in a smart home and deliver a comfortable life. Sensor data is composed of multiple sensitive information related to the user and appliances in the smart home. Here, we need to encrypt these data to protect our privacy.

3.2 IDENTITY-BASED AUTHENTICATION

Almost all smart home devices use an application through which they can be monitored or controlled like the MirAIe App for Panasonic AC, Smart Mi App for Smart Mi Kettle, and Universal Project remote control app for the classroom projectors of all models. These apps are connected to cloud storage or cloud services that ask for credentials for authentication.

A. Password Policies:

Smart home devices are authenticated based on the default password that comes from the manufacturer side. Almost 15% of these smart home devices still use default passwords. Devices not using a default password but using a weak password can be breached through a brute force attack using Hydra and a world list of possible usernames and passwords [2]. A list of 2117 default passwords of different models of 531 Vendors is available in the default password database on https://cirt.net/passwords and one default password of the Cisco Intrusion Detection System (IDS) is shown in Fig. 3.1 [3].

1. Cisco - *Cisco IDS*	
User ID	root
Password	attack
Level	Administrator
Doc	

Fig. 3.1. Default password of Cisco IDS

As an alternative to centralized authentication (e.g., Kerberos), researchers in [4], developed an authentication based on multiple devices. The system will authenticate the user even if one or more devices break down. That proved the robustness and greater availability of their smart home. The proposed scheme in [4] is a key confirmation-based authenticated key exchange protocol to use the benefits of a distributed IoT system. The client's password is shared among the smart home devices. Therefore, multiple devices and sensors verify and validate the user password.

B. Multi-Factor Authentication (MFA) in Smart Home

This communication in smart homes happens via insecure channels. That's why smart homes are vulnerable to many attacks. Therefore, a secure authentication protocol is used to send sensitive data within a smart home [5]. A secure IFTTT-based Smart Home framework uses a suitable captcha, and a One Time Password (OTP) authentication scheme [6]. The Elliptic Curve Cryptography (ECC) based two-factor user authentication for smart homes can resist all attacks on smart homes [7]. Secure smart home management access control uses multifactor authentication (MFA) mechanisms. MFA is not able to defend against insider threats, this research gap motivates researchers to integrate user behavior and environmental context to make intelligent authorization decisions. The system can be used to authenticate each interaction of the devices with a REST web service by using OTP. Secure Hash Algorithm 256 (SHA-256) authenticates all interaction with a Webserver with the help of an encrypted username, password, and token [8].

C. Cookies and Session ID:

The Diffie-Hellman (DH) key exchange protocol ensures the mutual authentication and session key establishment for secure communication. The standard IPv6 protocol provides authentication without any extra overhead cost. In [9], researchers modify the standard IPv6 interface identifier (IID). The unique identifier of 64-bit IID is generated from the user/owner's unique identification number and device identity. This scheme also provides session-key establishment using Diffie-Hellman (DH) key exchange public-key cryptography with the help of a unique 64-bit IID [9]. The simple cookies may be captured in the Storage section of Chrome Browser as shown in Fig. 3.2 and Fig. 3.3. In Fig. 3.2, the cookie name is login and values are test%2ftest.

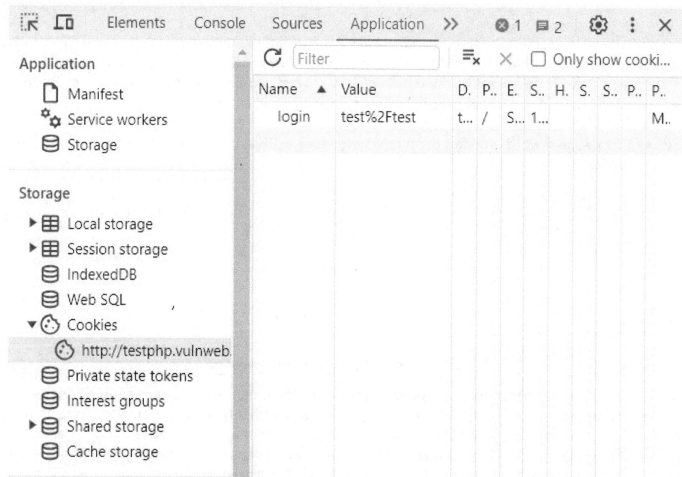

Fig. 2. Cookies of TestPHP Website Vulnerabilities

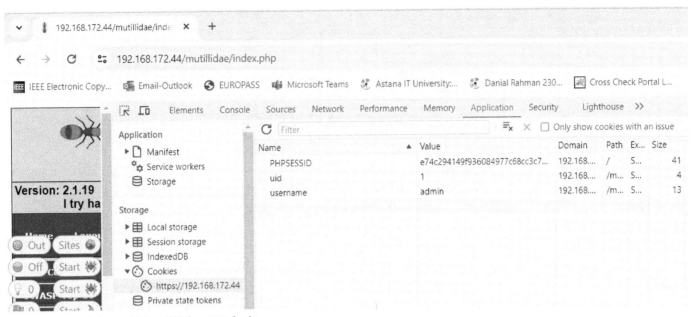

Fig. 3.3. Cookies of Mutillidae Website

In Fig. 3.3, the cookie's names are PHPSESSID, UID (User Identifier), and username. The value of cookie PHPSESSSID is an encrypted text whereas the value of UID and username is plain text. The cookie/session-based method is prone to session-stealing attacks and may also be insecure on unencrypted channels [10]. That's why in the next section, I am covering the application of encryption in smart homes.

3.3 ENCRYPTION

An intruder inside or a hacker nearer to the smart home usually targets wireless mediums used by smart home devices to get useful information about the users and violate user privacy. Researchers in [11] developed a methodology using a novel multi-stage privacy attack against user privacy to tackle this issue. Encryption is possible in Kali using a tool called keytool used to generate a 2,048-bit RSA (Rivest, Shamir, Adleman algorithm) key pair and self-signed certificate with a validity of 1,000 days as shown in Fig. 3.4. In [11], hackers also took advantage of the fact that while the encryption layer in the protocol protects only the payload of a packet, it fails to hide other information e.g., packet lengths, traffic rate of the network traffic. These metadata provide information to hackers about the messages exchanged.

```
┌──(kali㉿kali)-[~]
└─$ keytool -genkey -V -keystore key.keystore -alias hacked -keyalg RSA -keysize 2048 -validity 1000
Picked up _JAVA_OPTIONS: -Dawt.useSystemAAFontSettings=on -Dswing.aatext=true
Enter keystore password:
Re-enter new password:
What is your first and last name?
  [Unknown]:  Bishwajeet Pandey
What is the name of your organizational unit?
  [Unknown]:  Astana IT University
What is the name of your organization?
  [Unknown]:  Department of Intelligent System and Cyber Security
What is the name of your City or Locality?
  [Unknown]:  Astana
What is the name of your State or Province?
  [Unknown]:  Astana
What is the two-letter country code for this unit?
  [Unknown]:  KZ
Is CN=Bishwajeet Pandey, OU=Astana IT University, O="Department of Intelligent System and Cyber Security ", L=Astana, ST=Astana, C=KZ correct?
  [no]:  yes

Generating 2,048 bit RSA key pair and self-signed certificate (SHA256withRSA) with a validity of 1,000 days
        for: CN=Bishwajeet Pandey, OU=Astana IT University, O="Department of Intelligent System and Cyber Security ", L=Astana, ST=Astana, C=KZ
[Storing key.keystore]
```

Fig. 3.4. Generate a Key Pair and Key Store using the RSA Key Algorithm

The tool JARSIGNER is signing the Android application android_shell.apk using SHA1withRSA signature algorithm, SHA1 digest algorithm, and keystore generated by the KEYTOOL as shown in Fig. 3.5. The whole process is adding four META-INF files and signing AndroidManifest.xml, resources.arsc. and classes.dex.

```
┌──(kali㉿kali)-[~]
└─$ jarsigner -verbose -sigalg SHA1withRSA -digestalg SHA1 -keystore key.keystore android_shell.apk hacked
Picked up _JAVA_OPTIONS: -Dawt.useSystemAAFontSettings=on -Dswing.aatext=true
Enter Passphrase for keystore:
   adding: META-INF/MANIFEST.MF
   adding: META-INF/HACKED.SF
   adding: META-INF/HACKED.RSA
   adding: META-INF/SIGNFILE.SF
   adding: META-INF/SIGNFILE.RSA
  signing: AndroidManifest.xml
  signing: resources.arsc
  signing: classes.dex

>>> Signer
    X.509, CN=Bishwajeet Pandey, OU=Astana IT University, O="Department of Intelligent System and Cyber Security ", L=Astana, ST=Astana, C=KZ
    [trusted certificate]

jar signed.

Warning:
The signer's certificate is self-signed.
```

Fig. 3.5. Sign the Android application using SHA1withRSA signature and SHA1 digest

The JARSIGNER verifies the signature and certificate as shown in Fig.3.6.

```
┌──(kali㉿kali)-[~]
└─$ jarsigner -verify -verbose -certs android_shell.apk
Picked up _JAVA_OPTIONS: -Dawt.useSystemAAFontSettings=on -Dswing.aatext=true

        258 Sat Apr 06 10:41:30 EDT 2024 META-INF/MANIFEST.MF
        382 Sat Apr 06 10:51:34 EDT 2024 META-INF/HACKED.SF
       1557 Sat Apr 06 10:51:34 EDT 2024 META-INF/HACKED.RSA
        272 Sat Apr 06 10:41:30 EDT 2024 META-INF/SIGNFILE.SF
       1842 Sat Apr 06 10:41:30 EDT 2024 META-INF/SIGNFILE.RSA
          0 Sat Apr 06 10:41:30 EDT 2024 META-INF/
m ?    7112 Sat Apr 06 10:41:30 EDT 2024 AndroidManifest.xml
m ?     572 Sat Apr 06 10:41:30 EDT 2024 resources.arsc
m ?   20316 Sat Apr 06 10:41:30 EDT 2024 classes.dex

  s = signature was verified
  m = entry is listed in manifest
  k = at least one certificate was found in keystore
  ? = unsigned entry

- Signed by "CN=Bishwajeet Pandey, OU=Astana IT University, O="Department of Intelligent System and Cyber Security ", L=Astana, ST=Astana, C=KZ"
    Digest algorithm: SHA1 (disabled)
    Signature algorithm: SHA1withRSA (disabled), 2048-bit key
- Unparsable signature-related file META-INF/SIGNFILE.SF

WARNING: The jar will be treated as unsigned, because it is signed with a weak algorithm that is now disabled by the security property:

  jdk.jar.disabledAlgorithms=MD2, MD5, RSA keySize < 1024, DSA keySize < 1024, SHA1 denyAfter 2019-01-01, include jdk.disabled.namedCurves
```

Fig. 3.6. Verify the Signature and Certificate in Signed Android Apps

Zipalign is a tool included in the Android SDK. The tool Zipalign optimizes the packaging of an Android application (APK). The tool Zipalign also ensures that all uncompressed data starts with a particular byte alignment relative to the start of the file, which makes it possible for Android to access the application's resources more efficiently as shown in Fig. 3.7.

```
┌──(kali㉿kali)-[~]
└─$ zipalign -v 4 android_shell.apk signed_jar1.apk
Verifying alignment of signed_jar1.apk (4)...
      50 META-INF/MANIFEST.MF (OK - compressed)
     286 META-INF/HACKED.SF (OK - compressed)
     619 META-INF/HACKED.RSA (OK - compressed)
    1832 META-INF/ (OK)
    1882 META-INF/SIGNFILE.SF (OK - compressed)
    2162 META-INF/SIGNFILE.RSA (OK - compressed)
    3247 AndroidManifest.xml (OK - compressed)
    5067 resources.arsc (OK - compressed)
    5297 classes.dex (OK - compressed)
Verification successful
```

Fig. 3.7. Verify alignment of the signed Android application

In a smart home, attribute-based encryption (ABE) allows anyone to encrypt data for different recipients where only selected recipients whose attributes satisfy a given access policy will decrypt [12].

3.4 DIGITAL CERTIFICATES AND DIGITAL SIGNATURES

By leveraging digital certificates, smart home systems are enhancing their security, ensuring that devices and users are authenticated and that communication remains secure and trustworthy. A trusted Certificate Authority (CA) issues and manages digital certificates. The CA can be a third-party provider or managed by the smart home system provider itself. The Public Key Infrastructure (PKI)supports the creation, distribution, and management. It includes a set of roles, policies, and procedures required to create, distribute, manage, revoke, store, and use digital certificates. In [13], there is a self-built CA to provide a digital certificate to each user and each smart home controller and uses the SSL mutual authentication to verify the identity of the user and smart home controller. Digital Certificates are used for binding a public key with an identity and authenticity trusted by a third party, i.e., Certificate Authority (CA) over the internet. Digital certificates are suggested as a countermeasure to application-level attacks [14].

Fig. 3.8. Key Functions of Digital Certificate in Smart Home

Authentication, Secure Communication, Data Integrity, and Access Control are the four key functions of a Digital certificate in the Smart Home as shown in Fig. 8. Device authentication verifies that smart home appliances are not counterfeit or malicious devices. User authentication authenticates users accessing the smart home system. Digital Certificates enable encrypted communication between devices and between devices and the central smart home hub or cloud services. Digital Certificates help ensure that the data sent and received by smart home devices has not been altered. Digital certificates can be used to implement access control policies within the smart home ecosystem. In Fig. 9, we observe the usage of digital signature by a smart door lock.

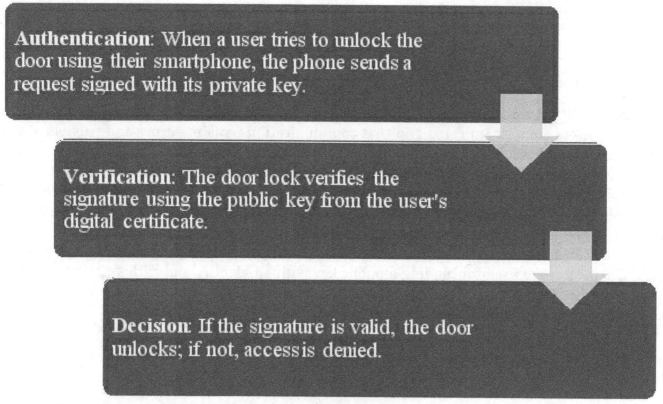

Authentication: When a user tries to unlock the door using their smartphone, the phone sends a request signed with its private key.

Verification: The door lock verifies the signature using the public key from the user's digital certificate.

Decision: If the signature is valid, the door unlocks; if not, access is denied.

Fig. 3.9. Door Lock Using Digital Signature in Smart Home

Fig. 3.10 is an example of generating a digital server certificate in the OWASP ZAP (Zed Attack Proxy) tool. There are options in ZAP to create a digital client certificate also.

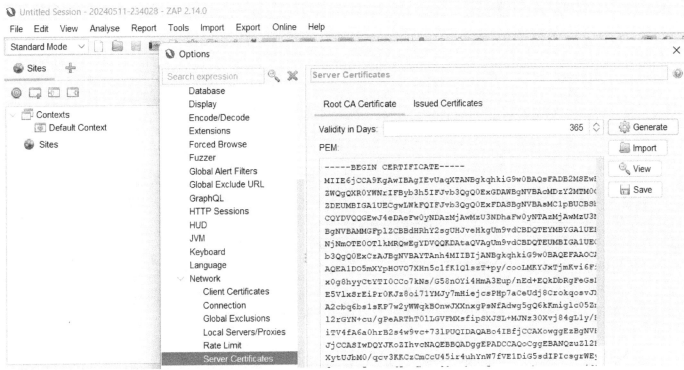

Fig. 3.10 Generation of Digital Certificate in OWASP ZAP

Managing HTTPS or SSL certificates and setting are easy in the Google Chrome browser as shown in Fig. 3.11.

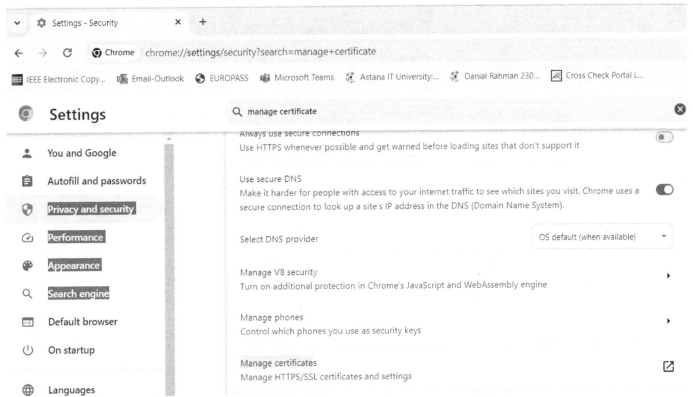

Fig. 3.11. Manage Certificates in Google Chrome

There are trusted root certification authorities, intermediate certification authorities are many other types of certifications in the Google Chrome browser as shown in Fig. 3.12.

Fig. 3.12. List of Certificates and Import New Certificate in Google Chrome Browser

3.5 CONCLUSION AND FUTURE SCOPE

Device authentication ensures that smart home appliances are genuine and not malicious. User authentication confirms the identity of users accessing the smart home system. Encrypted communication guarantees secure data exchange between devices and with the central smart home hub or cloud services. Digital certificates verify that data sent and received by smart home devices remains unaltered. Additionally, digital certificates are used to enforce access control policies within the smart home ecosystem.

REFERENCES

[1] Jhuang, Y. Y., Yan, Y. H., & Horng, G. J. (2023). GDPR Personal Privacy Security Mechanism for Smart Home System. *Electronics*, *12*(4), 831.

[2] Agazzi, A. E. (2020). Smart home, security concerns of IoT. *arXiv preprint arXiv:2007.02628*.

[3] Default Passwords, https://cirt.net/passwords

[4]Huszti, A., Kovács, S., & Oláh, N. (2022). Scalable, password-based and threshold authentication for smart homes. *International Journal of Information Security*, *21*(4), 707-723.

[5] Kaur, D., & Kumar, D. (2021). Cryptanalysis and improvement of a two-factor user authentication scheme for smart home. *Journal of Information Security and Applications*, *58*, 102787.

[6] Baruah, B., & Dhal, S. (2018). A two-factor authentication scheme against FDM attack in IFTTT-based Smart Home System. *Computers & Security*, *77*, 21-35.

[7] Zou, S., Cao, Q., Wang, C., Huang, Z., & Xu, G. (2021). A robust two-factor user authentication scheme-based ECC for smart home in IoT. *IEEE Systems Journal*, *16*(3), 4938-4949.

[8] Khoa, T. A., Nhu, L. M. B., Son, H. H., Trong, N. M., Phuc, C. H., Phuong, N. T. H., ... & Duc, D. N. M. (2020). Designing efficient smart home management with IoT smart lighting: a case study. *Wireless communications and mobile computing*, *2020*(1), 8896637.

[9] Kumar, P., & Chouhan, L. (2021). Design of secure session key using unique addressing and identification scheme for smart home Internet of Things network. *Transactions on Emerging Telecommunications Technologies*, *32*(5), e3993.

[10] Stolojescu-Crisan, C., Crisan, C., & Butunoi, B. P. (2021). An IoT-based smart home automation system. *Sensors*, *21*(11), 3784.

[11] Acar, A., Fereidooni, H., Abera, T., Sikder, A. K., Miettinen, M., Aksu, H., ... & Uluagac, S. (2020, July). Peek-a-boo: I see your smart home activities, even encrypted!. In *Proceedings of the 13th ACM Conference on Security and Privacy in Wireless and Mobile Networks* (pp. 207-218).

[12] Sicari, S., Rizzardi, A., Dini, G., Perazzo, P., La Manna, M., & Coen-Porisini, A. (2021). Attribute-based encryption and sticky policies for data access control in a smart home scenario: a comparison on networked smart object middleware. *International Journal of Information Security*, *20*, 695-713.

[13] Liu, Y., Zhang, G., Chen, W., & Wang, X. (2016, October). An efficient privacy protection solution for smart home application platform. In *2016 2nd IEEE International Conference on Computer and Communications (ICCC)* (pp. 2281-2285). IEEE.

[14] Mahmood, S., Gohar, M., Choi, J. G., Koh, S. J., Alquhayz, H., & Khan, M. (2021). Digital certificate verification scheme for smart grid using fog computing (FONICA). *Sustainability*, *13*(5), 2549.

GLOSSARY

H

Hardware Security Modules (HSM): The HSM is a dedicated hardware device that offers physical protection by integrating a new security layer into the system architecture

O

OWASP: The Open Web Application Security Project (OWASP) releases the top 10 vulnerabilities in Mobile, IoT, Websites, and so on.

P

PHPSESSID is a session cookie that is used to identify a user's session on a website. It is commonly used in PHP-based web applications to store a unique identifier for a user's session on the server. When a user visits a website that uses PHP sessions, a PHPSESSID cookie is sent to the user's browser and is stored on the user's computer. The server uses this cookie to identify the user's session and retrieve the appropriate data for that session. The PHPSESSID cookie is typically set to expire when the user closes their web browser.

S

Secure Enclaves: The Intel Software Guard Extensions (SGX) is the most popular secure enclaves that is referred as an isolated execution environments that provide a guarantee of the privacy of the data/code deployed inside it.

Smart Home Appliances: Smart home (SH) appliances can store data, respond to users' prompts, provide feedback to users, and issue alarms based on the data analytics of stored data.

T

Trusted Execution Environments (TEEs): TEEs are secure areas of central processors or devices that execute code with higher security than the rest of the device.

Trusted Platform Module (TPM): The TPM is a microchip (miniature System on a Chip (SoC)) developed by the Trusted Computing Group (TCG) that enhances the integrity of computing platforms.

W

Web Interface: Web interfaces provide a user-friendly way to control and monitor various smart devices through web browsers of computers, laptops, and smartphones. The web interface has multiple key aspects such as Data Encryption, Input Validation, Real-Time Control, Responsive Design, Notification and Alerts, Security, User-Friendly Design, and Intuitive Navigation.